STAR WARS™

REBEL HEROES

Written by Shari Last

Penguin Random House

Project Editor Shari Last
Designers Marcel Carry, Chris Gould, Lisa Rogers
Pre-production Producer Marc Staples
Senior Producer Alex Bell
Managing Editor Sadie Smith
Managing Art Editor Ron Stobbart
Art Director Lisa Lanzarini
Publisher Julie Ferris
Publishing Director Simon Beecroft

Reading Consultant Maureen Fernandes

For Lucasfilm
Editorial Assistant Samantha Holland
Image Unit Tim Mapp
Story Group Pablo Hidalgo, Leland Chee, Matt Martin
Creative Director of Publishing Michael Siglain

First published in Great Britain in 2017 by
Dorling Kindersley Limited
80 Strand, London WC2R 0RL
A Penguin Random House Company

10 9 8 7 6 5 4 3 2 1
001–298002–Jan/17

A CIP catalogue record for this book
is available from the British Library.

ISBN: 978-0-24128-002-7

Printed in China

Contents

The Empire

The galaxy used to be a peaceful place, but not anymore! It is now controlled by a fearsome government – the Empire.

One of the leaders of the Empire is Darth Vader, a terrifying warrior who wears a black mask and cloak. He leads an army of stormtroopers across the galaxy, forcing each planet to obey.

Only a few people are brave enough to rebel against the Empire.

These rebels are of different species and they come from all corners of the galaxy.

The rebels must be careful. Darth Vader and his scary stormtrooper army are searching for them!

Ezra Bridger

Ezra grew up on the planet Lothal, where he was a thief. One day he met a group of rebels. After going on a dangerous mission with them, Ezra decided to join their team.

Ezra is happy that he finally has a group of friends he can trust. He is learning to work as part of a team.

Ezra was surprised to learn that he has Force skills. Kanan Jarrus, one of his rebel teammates, is teaching him to become a Jedi.

Now that the rebel team is complete, they are ready to attack the Empire!

Kanan Jarrus

Kanan is a Jedi raised on the planet Coruscant. He is part of a team of rebel fighters. He is brave and strong-minded. Although Kanan lost his sight during a battle, he is more determined than ever to defeat the Empire.

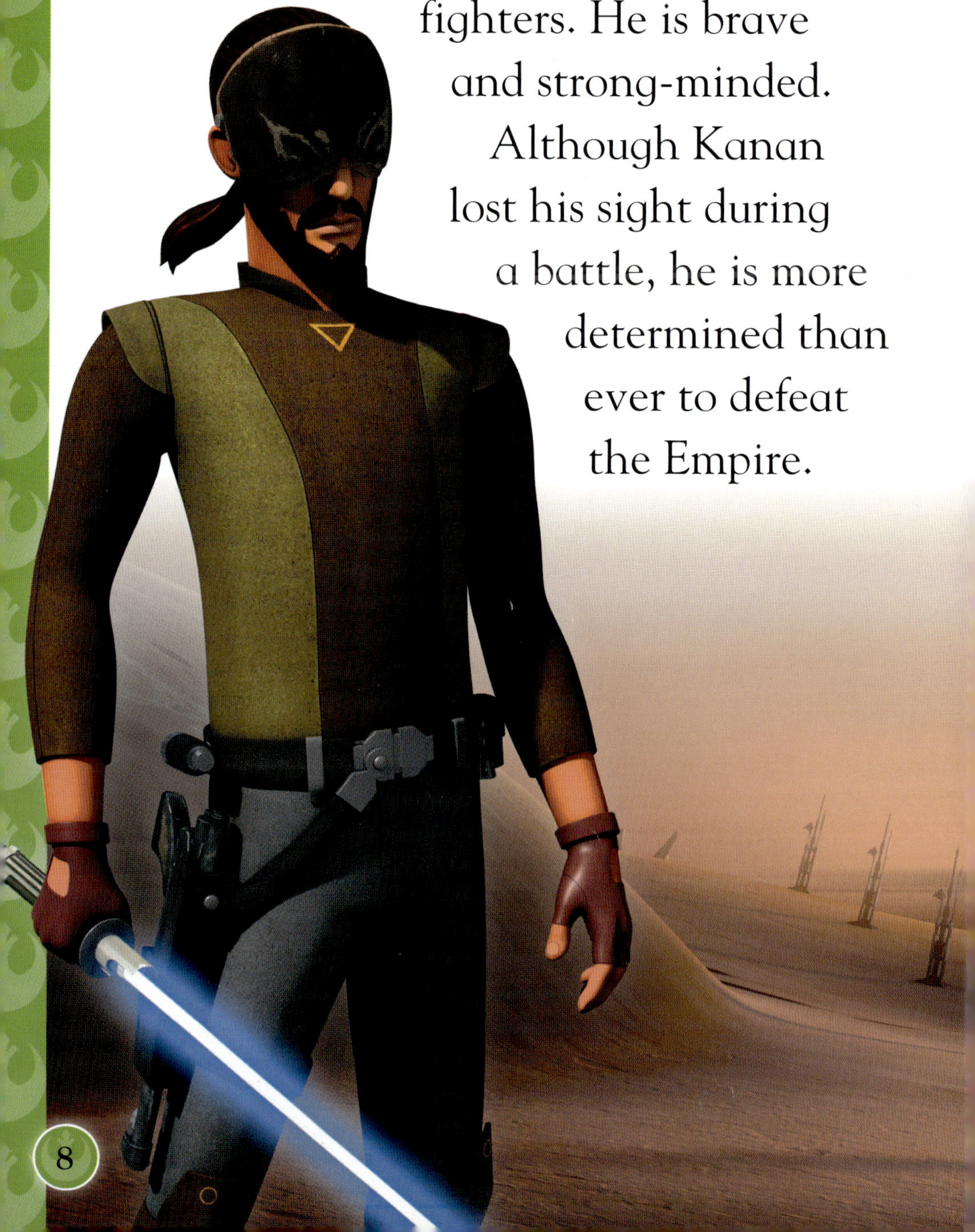

Hera Syndulla

Hera is a Twi'lek from the planet Ryloth. She is the leader of the rebels team and the pilot of their ship, the *Ghost*.

Hera is a great leader. She is not afraid of danger and always knows what to say to motivate her team.

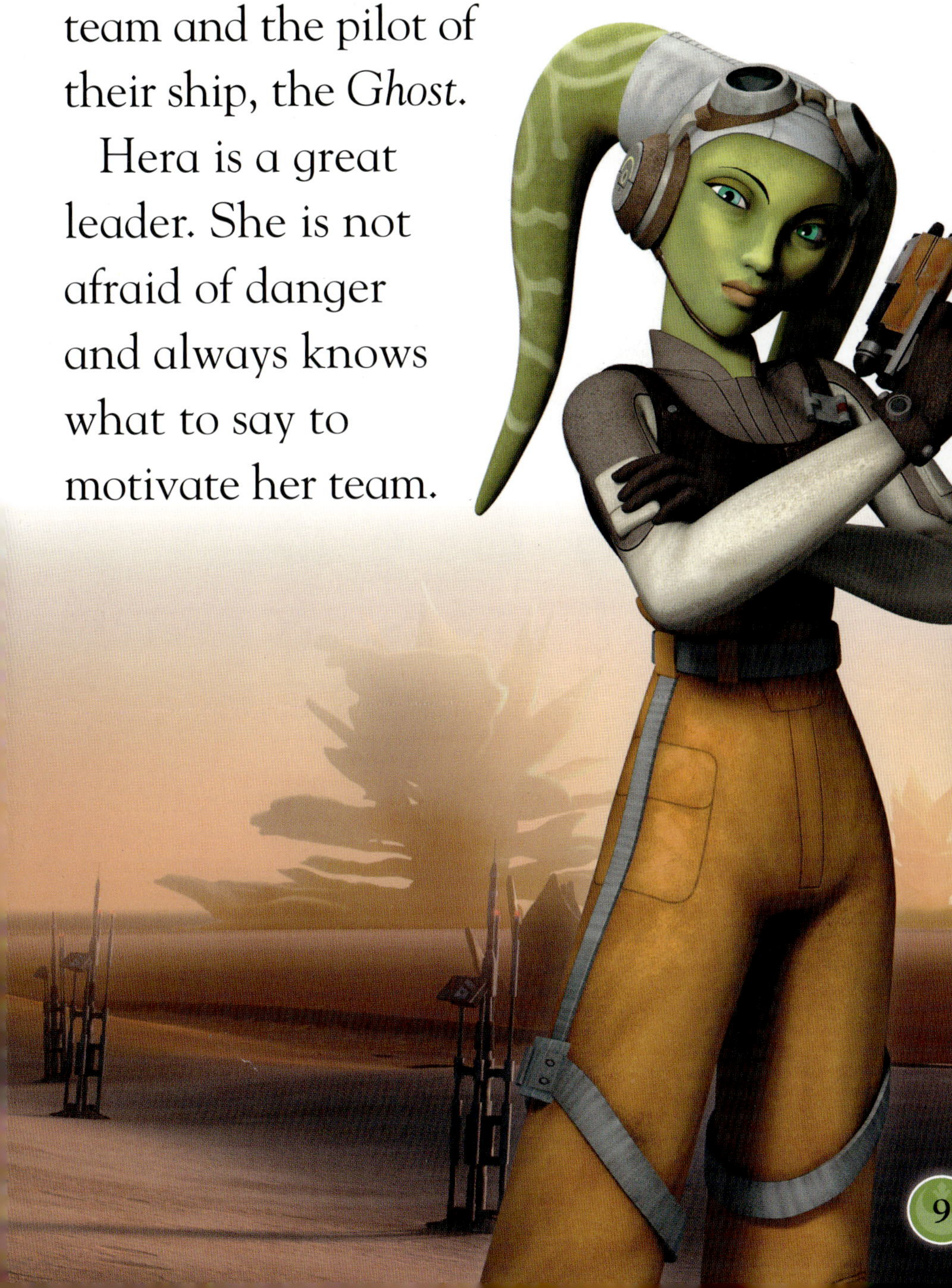

REBEL ALLIES

The rebels make many friends and allies during their missions to attack the Empire. Some of these allies are ready to join the Rebellion, while others wish to keep their involvement a secret.

Not Just a Clone

Rex used to be a clone trooper, but he was never controlled by the Empire. He had retired from a life of fighting until he met the *Ghost* crew. Now he is part of the team.

Imperial Defector

Tseebo is an Imperial Information Officer. He knows many, many secrets! He escaped from the Empire and brought the secrets to the *Ghost* crew. Will they trust him?

Good for Business

Smuggler Lando Calrissian can't always be trusted. Lando helps the rebels out, but only when he has something to gain! Still, he is useful for getting out of sticky situations.

Starship Builder

Quarrie is a mechanic who built a B-wing starfighter. Hera was the first to test it out. After the test, Quarrie joined the rebels and built a whole fleet of B-wings!

Imperial Ally

The Prime Minister of Lothal, Maketh Tua, believed in the Empire. However, when she realised how evil the Empire was, she did all she could to help the rebels.

Friendly Face

Jho is the owner of Old Jho's Pit Stop, a cantina on the planet Lothal. Jho is friends with the *Ghost* crew and he allows them to use his cantina as a safe place to hang out.

Senator with a Secret

Bail Organa is a well-known senator. Although he pretends to be loyal to the Empire, he secretly provides the rebels with starships, weapons and information.

Sabine Wren

Sabine is a brilliant weapons expert. She uses her knowledge to help her rebel team on board the *Ghost*.

Sabine grew up training to be an Imperial warrior. She soon realised the Empire was evil and left to join the rebels.

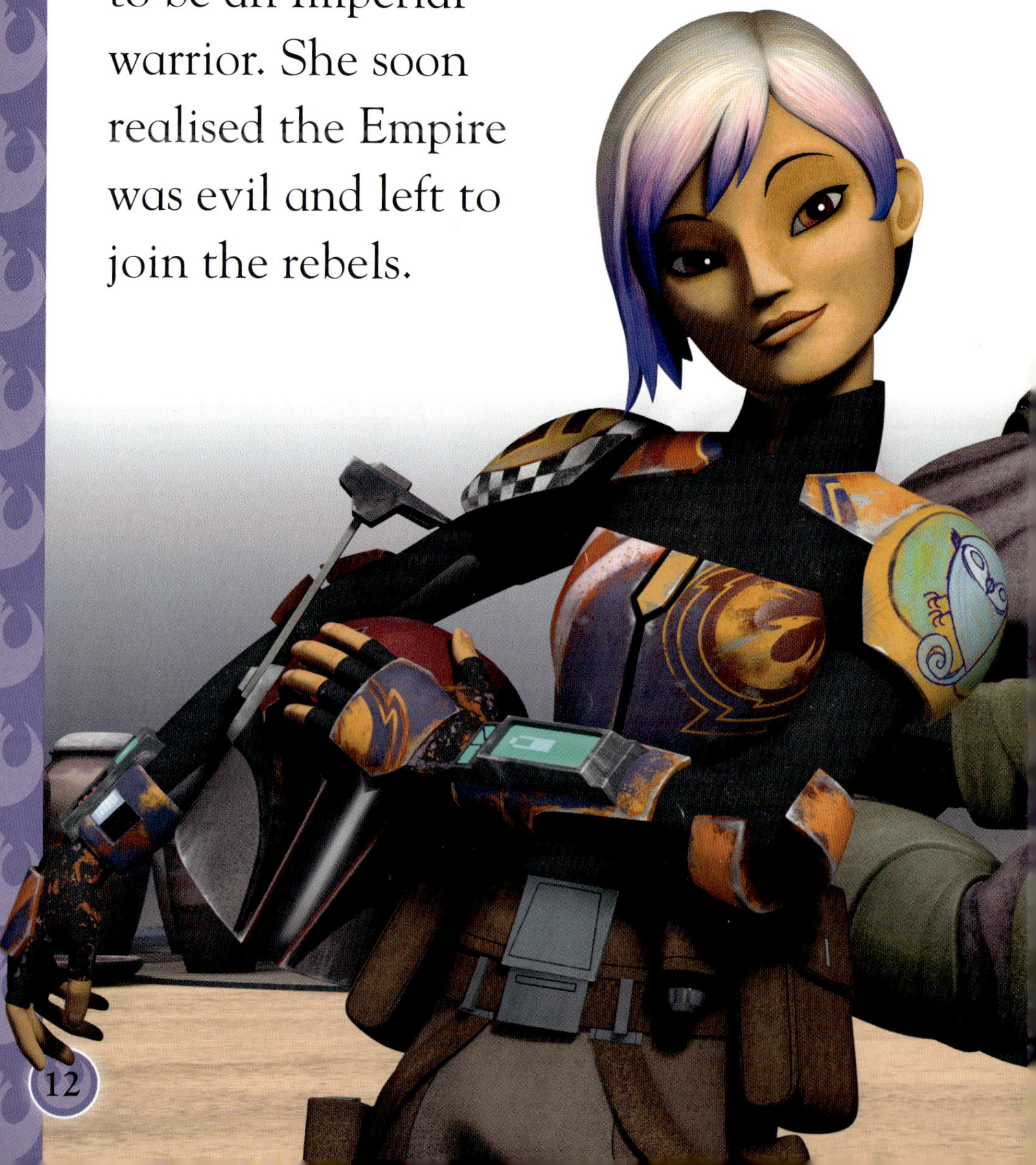

Zeb Orrelios

Known for his strength and fighting skills, Zeb Orrelios is the most fearsome member of the *Ghost* rebel crew.

Zeb used to be a captain on the planet Lasan. However, the Empire destroyed his home planet. Zeb wants to defeat the Empire once and for all.

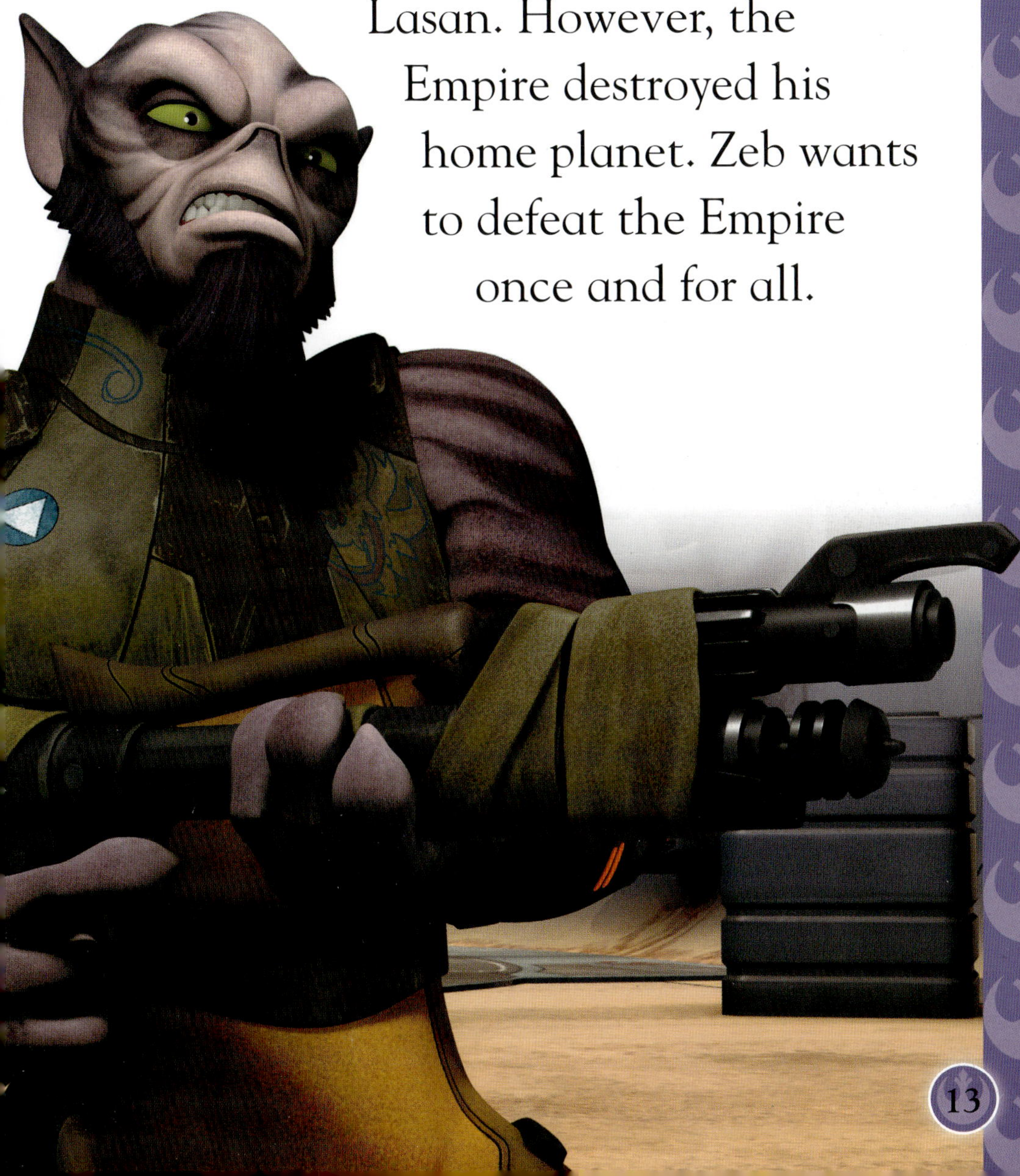

Ahsoka Tano

Ahsoka is a Togruta. She was raised on Coruscant. She trained as a Jedi warrior. However, Ahsoka made the difficult decision to leave the Jedi Order.

After the Empire was formed, Ahsoka became a very important rebel figure. She helps many rebel groups on their missions.

Ahsoka and Ezra discuss the best way to carry out their next mission.

Ahsoka has joined forces with the crew of the *Ghost* ship. She helps them with their plans to attack the Empire.

Ahsoka cares greatly about her new rebel friends. She takes an interest in Ezra's Jedi training. Ahsoka was once a Jedi, so she understands how difficult the training can be. She and Ezra soon become good friends.

Mission: Malachor

On the planet Malachor is an ancient Sith Temple. Ezra, Kanan and Ahsoka go to explore it. However, the mission leads Ezra down a dangerous path.

In the temple, Ezra meets a stranger. He is Darth Maul, an evil Sith warrior, in disguise. Together, they find a Sith Holocron. It contains many lost secrets of the Sith. Ezra wants to discover these secrets. He finds himself being drawn towards the dark side of the Force.

Kanan defeats Darth Maul to protect Ezra, but then Darth Vader arrives at the temple. Ahsoka uses her old Jedi lightsaber skills to battle Vader, giving Ezra and Kanan time to escape.

Ezra and Kanan return to their ship. However, Ezra cannot stop thinking about the dark side of the Force. Will he be able to stay true to the Jedi way?

Jyn Erso

Jyn is rebellious, but she is not a rebel… yet. While captured in an alien prison, Jyn is rescued by members of the Rebel Alliance. They need her help on an important mission to find her father.

Jyn has not seen her father, Galen, for many years. He has been forced to work for the Empire.

Jyn goes undercover during her mission with the Rebel Alliance.

Jyn agrees to join a team of rebels for this mission. The others quickly realise that Jyn doesn't always obey orders. However, Jyn is honest and wants justice more than anything. Her teammates decide to follow her as their leader.

REBEL STARSHIPS

POWERFUL STRIKE FIGHTER

A-WING

Length: 9.6 m (31.5 ft)

Top speed: 1,300 kph (808 mph)

Equipment: Defence shield, hyperdrive, laser cannons, concussion missiles

B-WING

BOMBER STARFIGHTER

Length: 16.9 m (55.5 ft)

Top speed: 950 kph (590 mph)

Equipment: Hyperdrive, laser cannons, proton torpedoes, ion cannon, composite beam laser

U-WING

TROOP TRANSPORT

Length: 25 m (82 ft)

Top speed: 950 kph (590 mph)

Equipment: Defence shield, hyperdrive, laser cannons

Y-WING

FIGHTER-BOMBER STARSHIP

Length: 23.4 m (77 ft)

Top speed: 1,000 kph (621 mph)

Equipment: Defence shield, hyperdrive, laser cannons, ion cannons, proton torpedo launchers

Length: 13.4 m (44 ft)

Top speed: 1,050 kph (652 mph)

Equipment: Laser cannons, proton torpedo launchers

ASSAULT STARFIGHTER

X-WING

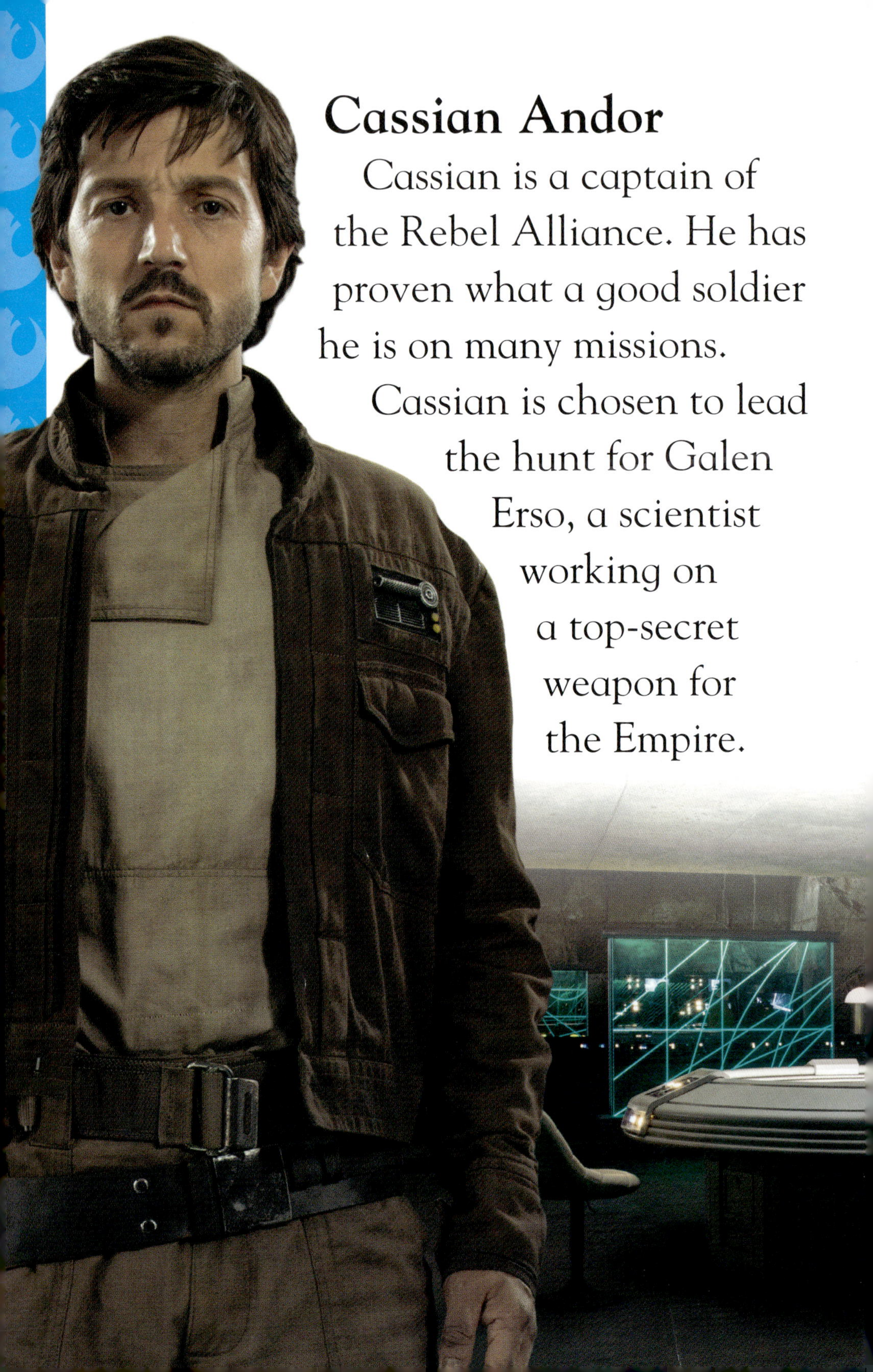

Cassian Andor

Cassian is a captain of the Rebel Alliance. He has proven what a good soldier he is on many missions.

Cassian is chosen to lead the hunt for Galen Erso, a scientist working on a top-secret weapon for the Empire.

Bodhi Rook

Bodhi used to be an Imperial pilot. When he discovered the Empire was building a top-secret weapon called the Death Star, he ran away.

Bodhi shared what he knows with the Rebel Alliance. He is now part of the mission to gather information about the Death Star. Bodhi's piloting and computer skills are useful for the mission.

Bodhi hacks into Imperial systems during the mission.

Chirrut Îmwe

Chirrut is a warrior monk. He might be blind, but he has trained his mind and body to develop fast reflexes.

Chirrut helps Jyn and Cassian escape when they are being chased by stormtroopers on the moon of Jedha. He decides to join forces with the rebels.

Baze Malbus

Baze lives on the moon Jedha, which is under Imperial control. Baze will do everything he can to attack the Empire.

Baze and Chirrut are old friends, although they sometimes disagree about things. However, they both agree to join the Rebel Alliance.

Mission: Scarif

Jyn and her team have learned a dangerous secret: there is a way to destroy the Death Star! To find out how, they must travel to the planet Scarif and steal the Death Star plans.

Scarif is a tropical planet, patrolled by giant Imperial walking machines.

AT-ACT walkers patrol the beaches of Scarif.

Cassian and Jyn wear Imperial disguises to get past security on Scarif.

The team use all their skills to locate and steal the Death Star plans. However, the Empire has many forces on Scarif, ready to stop Jyn's mission.

Will the team be able to pass the plans on to the Rebel Alliance in time?

Luke Skywalker

Luke Skywalker grew up on a small farm. He is now a famous hero of the Rebel Alliance!

Luke is known for his fast reflexes, loyalty and pilot skills. He once received a medal for helping the rebels destroy the Empire's greatest weapon, the Death Star.

Luke is also the last Jedi in the galaxy. He works very hard at his Jedi training.

Luke flies an X-wing on his way to attack the Death Star.

When Luke discovers his father is Darth Vader, he is shocked. However, Luke stays true to the rebel cause and helps destroy the Empire.

Years later, Luke starts to train young Jedi, but he mysteriously disappears. Where could Luke Skywalker be hiding?

Mission: Echo Base

The Rebel Alliance's secret base has been discovered. Darth Vader and his army are on their way!

Luke Skywalker and the rebel troops defend Echo Base. They fire ion cannons and launch snowspeeders.

Meanwhile, Darth Vader leads his army of snowtroopers. Enormous AT-AT walkers stomp across the icy plains of Hoth, shooting deadly blaster fire.

The rebels are brave and strong, but Vader has taken them by surprise. Echo Base is destroyed and the rebels are forced to run away.

Hoth is a cold, icy planet. Rebel troops have to wear cold-weather gear.

REBEL LEGENDS

Some rebels are famous for their heroic deeds. Yoda and Obi-Wan Kenobi are known throughout the galaxy as two of the most legendary members of the Rebel Alliance.

Yoda

Yoda is the Grand Jedi Master. He has trained many Jedi warriors. When the Empire takes control, Yoda goes into hiding. Years later, he teaches Luke Skywalker the ways of the Jedi – training that will lead to a rebel victory.

Obi-Wan Kenobi

Obi-Wan is a famous Jedi Master. After many years in hiding from the Empire, he joins the rebels on their mission to destroy the Death Star. He battles Darth Vader, helping the others to escape.

Leia Organa

Leia Organa is an important member of the Rebel Alliance.

Leia is also a senator and she tries to solve problems peacefully. However, she is always ready to jump into battle to defend the galaxy from danger.

Thanks to Leia, the rebels are able to destroy the Empire's most deadly weapon: the Death Star.

Years after the Rebel Alliance is disbanded, a new threat faces the galaxy: the First Order. The First Order is just as evil as the Empire was.

Leia forms the Resistance to fight back against the First Order. Many new rebels join the Resistance. Leia leads the Resistance as a general.

C-3PO, Admiral Statura and General Organa plan missions from Resistance HQ.

Chewbacca

This tall, hairy Wookiee has been on many dangerous missions with the Rebel Alliance and the Resistance.

Hardly anything scares Chewbacca. Actually, most of his enemies are afraid of him! He is a fierce warrior, expert pilot and loyal friend.

Han Solo

Han Solo is a famous general from the days of the Rebel Alliance. He is the pilot of the *Millennium Falcon*, one of the fastest starships in the galaxy!

With his co-pilot and best friend, Chewbacca, Han later joins the Resistance and continues to fight for freedom.

MILLENNIUM FALCON

The *Millennium Falcon* is a famous starship, owned by Han Solo. The *Falcon* has seen many adventures and been in lots of battles. It might need a few repairs, but it is still one of the fastest ships in the galaxy.

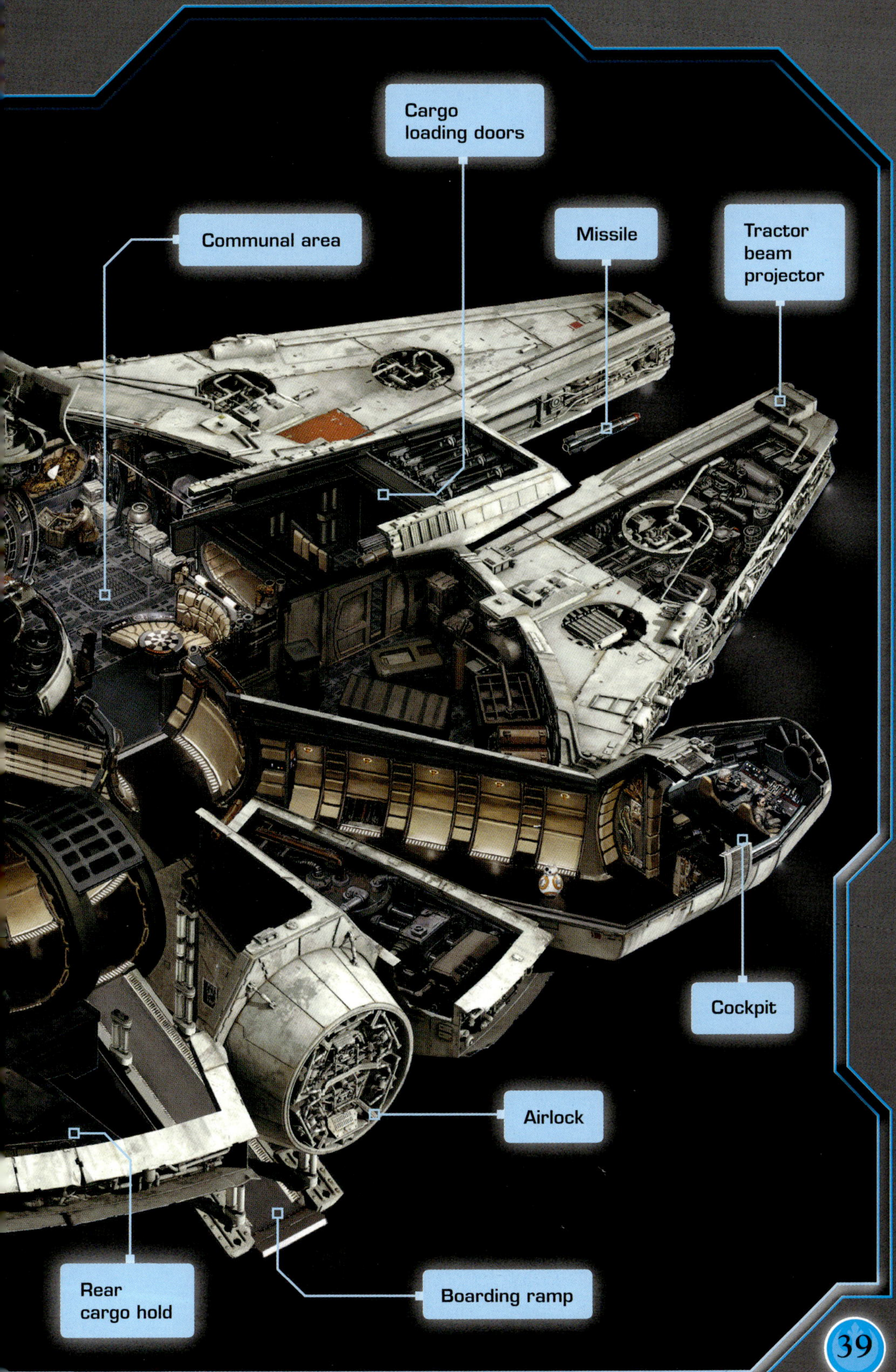
Cargo loading doors
Communal area
Missile
Tractor beam projector
Cockpit
Airlock
Rear cargo hold
Boarding ramp

Mon Mothma

Leading the Rebel Alliance is difficult, but Mon Mothma is perfect for the job. She is a calm leader, able to unite all the rebels against their enemy: the Empire.

Mon Mothma knows when to negotiate and when to battle. Most importantly, Mon Mothma truly believes in the rebel mission for freedom across the galaxy.

Admiral Ackbar

Admiral Ackbar commands the rebel fleet. He plays an important role in the destruction of the Empire.

Years after the end of the Empire, Ackbar is a member of the Resistance. He uses his years of battle experience to help the Resistance plan its attack on the First Order.

STAR PILOTS

Battles can be won or lost depending on the skills of the pilots. Both the Rebel Alliance and the Resistance rely on their pilots to soar to victory!

LUKE SKYWALKER

Homeworld: Tatooine

Rank: Commander, Rebel Alliance

Squadron: Red Squadron

Call sign: Red Five

Special skills: Fast reflexes

NIEN NUNB

Homeworld: Sullust

Rank: Lieutenant Commander, Resistance

Special skills: Navigation

Rebel pilots prepare the starships for their mission.

BIGGS DARKLIGHTER

Homeworld: Tatooine

Rank: Officer, Rebel Alliance

Squadron: Red Squadron

Call sign: Red Three

Special skills: Flying through narrow spaces

SNAP WEXLEY

Homeworld: Akiva

Rank: Captain, Resistance

Squadron: Blue Squadron

Special skills: Scouting and fact-finding

Mission: Death Star

The Empire's new Death Star is even bigger than the old one! It is almost complete, which means it will soon be able to destroy any planet in the galaxy.

The Rebel Alliance has planned a mission to destroy the Death Star. First, they must destroy the Death Star's protective energy shield.

Nien Nunb and Lando Calrissian fly the *Millennium Falcon*.

The rebel fleet is speeding towards the Death Star, ready to attack. A new radio message reveals that the shield is down! Rebel General Lando Calrissian flies the *Millennium Falcon* into battle. He proves his loyalty to the rebel cause by flying into the Death Star and striking at its core. The Death Star explodes!

The First Order

After the destruction of the Death Star, the Empire fell apart. The First Order has taken its place. The First Order is a dangerous organisation. Its leaders want to take control of the galaxy.

Kylo Ren is a scary First Order warrior. He leads stormtroopers across the galaxy.

Thousands of stormtroopers at Starkiller Base, the First Order's headquarters.

The stormtroopers attack anyone who does not support the First Order.

There is a small group of brave people who want to rebel against the First Order. They are called the Resistance.

Kylo Ren

SECRET BASES

A secret HQ needs to be somewhere safe from enemy spies. The Rebel Alliance and the Resistance know that some day their bases will be discovered. They are always on the lookout for a good location for their next base.

RESISTANCE BASE, D'QAR
The planet D'Qar has a good water supply and is not close to important trade routes. The Resistance base is disguised under grass-covered hills.

HOME ONE
This star cruiser became the Rebel Alliance base after Echo Base was destroyed. A mobile headquarters has its advantages, because it can change location to avoid detection.

ECHO BASE, HOTH
The Rebel Alliance built Echo Base on the ice planet Hoth. Hoth is uninhabited, making it easier to keep the base secret from the Empire.

REBEL BASE, YAVIN 4
The jungle moon of Yavin 4 is home to a crumbling ancient temple. The Rebel Alliance built its headquarters inside the temple. It was big enough to house all their spaceships.

PHOENIX HOME
This starship is a mobile base for various rebel groups, including the *Ghost* crew. New missions are planned in its command centre.

"ECHO STATION 3-T-8, WE HAVE SPOTTED IMPERIAL WALKERS!"

ECHO BASE OFFICER

Poe Dameron

Poe Dameron is one of the bravest pilots in the Resistance! He is smart, daring and always prepared to undertake a dangerous mission.

Poe is fiercely loyal to the Resistance. He is proud to serve under General Leia Organa, a rebel hero he truly admires.

Whenever the Resistance needs a star pilot, they turn to Poe. His X-wing starfighter is one of the fastest ships in the Resistance fleet.

When the Resistance asks Poe to search for the missing hero, Luke Skywalker, Poe is incredibly honoured.

Poe's black-and-orange X-wing is called *Black One*.

DARING

BB-8

BB-8 is an astromech droid. He helps Poe fly his X-wing starfighter. BB-8 is very loyal. He will travel for miles to help his master.

Chopper

Chopper can be grumpy, but he loves playing tricks on his friends! He is also excellent at repairing starships.

R2-D2

Cheeky R2-D2 is an astromech droid. He helps fly and fix starships. R2-D2 is not afraid of anything!

DROIDS

Rusty, shiny, round or tall, droids are heroes too! The Rebel Alliance and Resistance owe many of their victories to their mechanical allies.

C-3PO
C-3PO is a clever protocol droid. He might be a bit scared about going into battle, but he is always loyal to his masters.

K-2SO
This tall security droid looks scary, and he can be! He is, however, loyal to the rebels and will do whatever he can to help.

Rey

Rey lived alone on the planet Jakku, until she met a Resistance droid named BB-8. Rey used her talents as a warrior and a pilot to help BB-8 escape from stormtroopers. She was surprised to discover that she has strong Force powers.

Now a member of the Resistance, Rey is ready to defend the galaxy.

Finn

Finn used to be a First Order stormtrooper known as FN-2187. During a battle, he saw how cruel the First Order was, so he ran away.

Now a member of the Resistance, Finn fights against the First Order. He joins Rey, Han Solo and Chewbacca on a mission to destroy Starkiller Base.

Mission: Starkiller Base

The headquarters of the First Order is a huge planet called Starkiller Base. Starkiller Base is a deadly weapon. It can wipe out several planets at once! The Resistance are going to destroy it.

Rey was a prisoner on Starkiller Base, but she escaped. She wants to help the Resistance fleet get close enough to the planet so they can begin their attack.

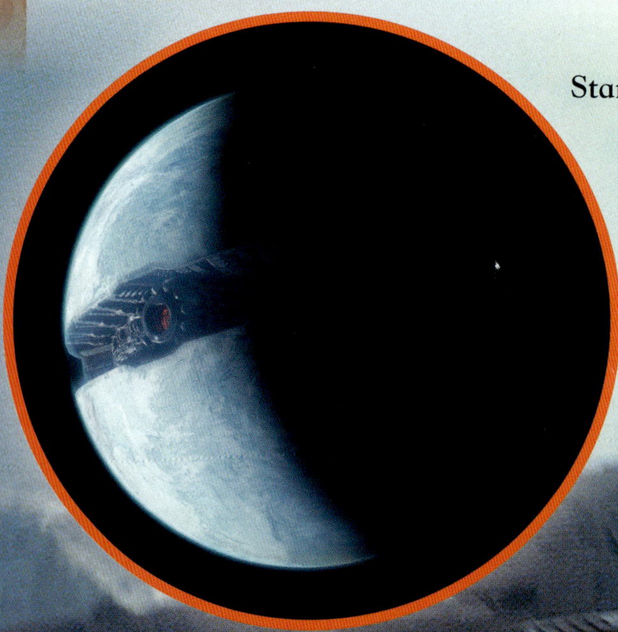

Starkiller Base

Finn, Chewbacca and Han Solo sneak into Starkiller Base. They find Rey, and plant lots of explosives.

When the explosives go off, Poe is able to lead the Resistance fleet into battle above the surface of the planet. While the starships attack, Poe flies his X-wing into the base and destroys it from within. Starkiller Base explodes! The galaxy is safe once more.

Quiz

1. Who is teaching Ezra to be a Jedi?

2. Who is the pilot of the *Ghost*?

3. On which planet do Ezra, Kanan and Ahsoka discover a Sith Temple?

4. What is the name of Jyn Erso's father?

5. What do Jyn and her team want to steal from the planet Scarif?

6. Which rebel hero went missing?

7. What is the name of the rebel base on the planet Hoth?

8. Who is the leader of the Resistance?

9. What starfighter does Poe Dameron fly?

10. Which Resistance hero used to be a stormtrooper?

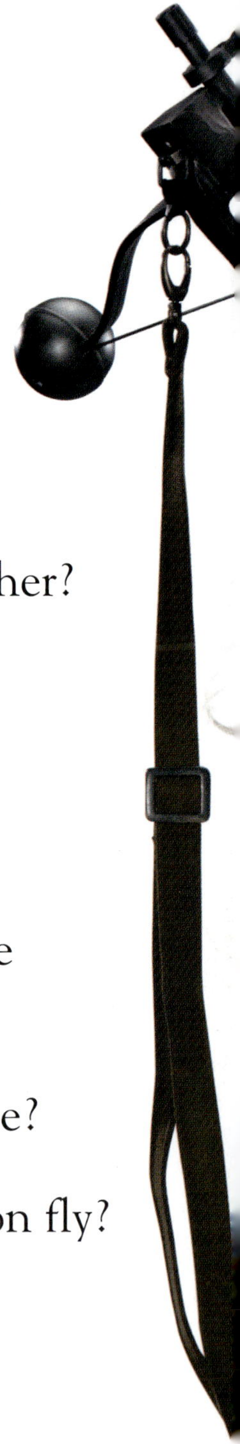

Answers on page 64

Glossary

astromech droid
A robot who helps fly and repair starships.

cantina
A bar where smugglers and criminals like to hang out.

Force
A mysterious energy that has a light side and a dark side. It can be used for good or for evil.

government
A group that rules over the rest of the people.

Holocron
An object that stores important information.

hyperdrive
A machine that allows starships to travel through space at the speed of light.

Jedi
A warrior who uses the light side of the Force to seek justice.

lightsaber
A sword that has a glowing blade of energy.

motivate
To give someone a reason for doing something.

negotiate
To come to an agreement through discussion.

protocol droid
A robot who helps with communications.

rebel
A person who opposes the organisation in power.

Rebel Alliance
A group created to oppose the rule of the Empire.

Resistance
A group created to protect the galaxy from the First Order.

senator
A politician who speaks on behalf of his or her planet.

Sith
An evil person who uses the dark side of the Force to gain power.

Guide for Parents

This book is part of an exciting four-level reading series for children, developing the habit of reading widely for both pleasure and information. These chapter books have a compelling main narrative to suit your child's reading ability. Each book is designed to develop your child's reading skills, fluency, grammar awareness and comprehension in order to build confidence and engagement when reading.

Ready for a *Level* 3 book

YOUR CHILD SHOULD

- be able to read most words without needing to stop and break them down into sound parts.
- read smoothly, in phrases and with expression. By this level, your child will be mostly reading silently.
- self-correct when some word or sentence doesn't sound right.

A VALUABLE AND SHARED READING EXPERIENCE

For some children, text reading, particularly non-fiction, requires much effort but adult participation can make this both fun and easier. So here are a few tips on how to use this book with your child.

TIP 1 **Check out the contents together before your child begins:**

- invite your child to check the back cover text, contents page and layout of the book and comment on it.
- ask your child to make predictions about the story.
- chat about the information your child might want to find out.

TIP 2 **Encourage fluent and flexible reading:**

- support your child to read in fluent, expressive phrases, making full use of punctuation and thinking about the meaning.

- encourage your child to slow down and check information where appropriate.

TIP 3 Indicators that your child is reading for meaning:

- your child will be responding to the text if he/she is self-correcting and varying his/her voice.
- your child will want to chat about what he/she is reading or is eager to turn the page to find out what will happen next.

TIP 4 Praise, share and chat:

- encourage your child to recall specific details after each chapter.
- provide opportunities for your child to pick out interesting words and discuss what they mean.
- discuss how the author captures the reader's interest.
- ask questions about the text. These help to develop comprehension skills and awareness of the language used.

A FEW ADDITIONAL TIPS

- Read to your child regularly to demonstrate fluency, phrasing and expression; to find out or check information; and for sharing enjoyment.
- Encourage your child to reread favourite texts to increase reading confidence and fluency.
- Check that your child is reading a range of different types, such as poems, jokes and following instructions.

Index

Answers to the quiz on page 58:
1. Kanan Jarrus 2. Hera Syndulla 3. Malachor
4. Galen Erso 5. the Death Star plans 6. Luke Skywalker
7. General Leia Organa 8. Echo Base 9. X-wing 10. Finn